This book belongs to:

_____

Ramadan is the month in which Allah Almighty opens His doors of mercy, forgiveness and blessings upon Muslims. This month is anxiously awaited by all the Muslims as they perform the duty of fasting in this month.

Making Dua in this Holy Month is one of the major deeds Muslims do to invoke Allah and seek His blessings. Therefore, besides the general Ramadan Duas, there are other supplications that Muslims can recite while fasting. In that regard, this booklet was made in order to compile 30 Ramadan supplications for 30 days of Ramadan for its readers. You can daily consult each Dua to call upon Allah in a unique way.

Wishing you all a blessed month!

Day 1

اَللّـهُمَّ اجْعَلْ صِيامي فيهِ صِيامَ الصّائِمينَ، وَقِيامي فيهِ قِيامَ
الْقائِمينَ، وَنَبِّهْني فيهِ عَنْ نَوْمَةِ الْغافِلينَ، وَهَبْ لى جُرْمي
فيهِ يا اِلـهَ الْعالَمينَ، وَاعْفُ عَنّي يا عافِياً عَنْ الْمجْرِمينَ

Lord! Make my fast in it one of those who truly fast,

my prayers those of who truly pray, and awaken me

from the sleep of the inattentive, grant me

forgiveness for my sins in it, O Lord of the Worlds,

and do forgive me, O One Who forgives criminals

Prayer tracker

Fajr ☐

Dhur ☐

Asr ☐

tarawih ☐

Maghrib ☐

Isha'a ☐

Nawafel ☐

Day 2

اَللّٰهُمَّ قَرِّبْني فيهِ اِلى مَرْضاتِكَ، وَجَنِّبْني فيهِ مِنْ سَخَطِكَ وَنَقِماتِكَ، وَوَفِّقْني فيهِ لِقِرآءَةِ آياتِكَ بِرَحْمَتِكَ يا اَرْحَمَ الرّاحِمينَ

Lord! Bring me closer in it to Your pleasure, enable me in it to avoid Your anger and wrath, enable me to be in it to recite Your verses with Your mercy, O most merciful of those who have mercy!

Prayer tracker

Fajr ☐

Dhur ☐

Asr ☐

tarawih ☐

Maghrib ☐

Isha'a ☐

Nawafel ☐

Day 3

اَللّـهُمَّ ارْزُقْني فيهِ الذِّهْنَ وَالتَّنْبيهَ ، وَباعِدْني فيهِ مِنَ السَّفاهَةِ وَالتَّمْويهِ ، وَاجْعَلْ لى نَصيباً مِنْ كُلِّ خَيْر تُنْزِلُ فيهِ، بِجُودِكَ يا أجود الْأَجْوَدينَ

Lord! Grant me in it intelligence and attentiveness,

distance me in it from nonsense and concealment,

allot for me a portion of everything good which You

send down in it with Your generosity, O most

generous One!

Prayer tracker

Fajr ☐

Dhur ☐

Asr ☐

tarawih ☐

Maghrib ☐

Isha'a ☐

Nawafel ☐

Day 4

اَللّٰهُمَّ قَوِّني فيهِ عَلى إقامة أمرك، وأذقني فيهِ حَلاوَةَ
ذِكْرِكَ، وَأَوْزِعْني فيهِ لِاداءِ شُكْرِكَ بِكَرَمِكَ، وَاحْفَظْني
فيهِ بِحِفْظِكَ وَسَتْرِكَ، يا أبصر النَّاظِرينَ

Lord! Strengthen me in it to perform Your commands,
enable me in it to taste the sweetness of mentioning
Your Name, enable me in it to truly thank You with
Your generosity, and safeguard me in it with Your
safeguard and cover, O most seeing One!

Prayer tracker

Fajr ☐

Dhur ☐

Asr ☐

tarawih ☐

Maghrib ☐

Isha'a ☐

Nawafel ☐

Day 5

اَللّـهُمَّ اجْعَلْني فيهِ مِنَ الْمُسْتَغْفِرينَ، وَاجْعَلْني فيهِ مِنْ
عِبادِكَ الصّالِحينَ ألْقانِتينَ ، وَاجْعَلني فيهِ مِنْ اَوْلِيائِكَ
الْمُقَرَّبينَ، بِرَأْفَتِكَ يا اَرْحَمَ الرّاحِمينَ

Lord! Enable me in it to be among those who seek

Your forgiveness, make me in it among Your righteous

and adoring servants, and enable me to be one of Your

close friends through Your compassion, O most

merciful One!

Prayer tracker

Fajr	☐		
Dhur	☐	Maghrib	☐
Asr	☐	Isha'a	☐
tarawih	☐	Nawafel	☐

Day 6

اللّـهُمَّ لا تَخْذُلْني فيهِ لِتَعَرُّضِ مَعْصِيَتِكَ، وَلا تَضْرِبْني
بِسِياطِ نَقِمَتِكَ، وَزَحْزِحْني فيهِ مِنْ مُوجِباتِ سَخَطِكَ ،
بِمَنِّكَ وأياديك يا مُنْتَهى رَغْبَةِ الرّاغِبينَ

Lord! Do not abandon me in it when I am exposed to

transgressing Your limits, do not whip me with the whips

of Your wrath, keep me away from whatever brings

about Your anger with Your boons and assistance, O One

Who is the ultimate end of the desirous

Prayer tracker

Fajr ☐

Dhur ☐

Asr ☐

tarawih ☐

Maghrib ☐

Isha'a ☐

Nawafel ☐

Day 7

اَللَّـهُمَّ اَعِنّي فِيهِ عَلى صِيامِهِ وَقِيامِهِ، وَجَنِّبْني فيهِ مِنْ هَفَواتِهِ وَآثامِهِ، وَارْزُقْني فيهِ ذِكْرَكَ بِدَوامِهِ، بِتَوْفيقِكَ يا هادِيَ الْمُضِلّينَ

Lord! Help me in it to fast and to pray as it is worth, help me avoid its slips and sins, and grant me in it to continuously remember You with Your enabling, O One Who guides those who stray!

Prayer tracker

Fajr ☐

Dhur ☐

Asr ☐

tarawih ☐

Maghrib ☐

Isha'a ☐

Nawafel ☐

Day 8

اَللّـهُمَّ ارْزُقْني فيهِ رَحْمَةَ الأيتامِ، وإطعام اَلطَّعامِ،
وإفشاء السَّلامِ، وَصُحْبَةَ الْكِرامِ، بِطَوْلِكَ يا ملجأ الآملين

Lord! Grant me in it mercy due to orphans, to be able to
give away food, to disseminate the peace, to accompany
the good ones through Your own favors, O haven of the
hopeful!

Prayer tracker

Fajr ☐

Dhur ☐

Asr ☐

tarawih ☐

Maghrib ☐

Isha'a ☐

Nawafel ☐

Day 9

اللَّهُمَّ اجْعَلْ لي فيهِ نَصيباً مِنْ رَحْمَتِكَ الْواسِعَةِ،
وَاهْدِني فيهِ لِبَراهينِكَ السّاطِعَةِ، وَخُذْ بِناصِيَتي إلى
مَرْضاتِكَ الْجامِعَةِ، بِمَحَبَّتِكَ يا أمل الْمُشْتاقينَ

Lord! Allot for me in it a portion of Your spacious
mercy, guide me in it to Your glittering proofs, take
my forelock to whatever achieves Your collective
Pleasure through Your love, O hope of the eager ones!

Prayer tracker

Fajr ☐

Dhur ☐

Asr ☐

tarawih ☐

Maghrib ☐

Isha'a ☐

Nawafel ☐

Day 10

اَللّـهُمَّ اجْعَلْني فيهِ مِنَ الْمُتَوَكِّلينَ عَلَيْكَ، وَاجْعَلْني فيهِ
مِنَ الْفائِزينَ لَدَيْكَ، وَاجْعَلْني فيهِ مِنَ الْمُقَرَّبينَ اِلَيْكَ،
بِإحسانك يا غايَةَ الطّالِبينَ

Lord! Make me in it among those who depend on
You, make me in it among the winners, and make me
in it among those who are close to You with Your
kindness, O ultimate end of the seekers!

Prayer tracker

Fajr ☐

Dhur ☐

Asr ☐

tarawih ☐

Maghrib ☐

Isha'a ☐

Nawafel ☐

Day 11

اَللّـهُمَّ حَبِّبْ اِلَيَّ فيهِ الإحسانَ، وَكَرِّهْ اِلَيَّ فيهِ الْفُسُوقَ وَالْعِصْيانَ، وَحَرِّمْ عَلَيَّ فيهِ السَّخَطَ وَالنّيرانَ بِعَوْنِكَ يا غِياثَ الْمُسْتَغيثينَ

Lord! Make me in it love benevolence, hate immorality and rebellion, and prohibit in it anger against me and the Fires with Your assistance, O One Who brings relief to those who plead for it!

Prayer tracker

Fajr ☐

Dhur ☐

Asr ☐

tarawih ☐

Maghrib ☐

Isha'a ☐

Nawafel ☐

Day 12

اَللّـهُمَّ زَيِّنّي فيهِ بِالسِّتْرِ وَالْعَفافِ، وَاسْتُرْني فيهِ بِلِباسِ الْقُنُوعِ وَالْكَفافِ، وَاحْمِلْني فيهِ عَلَى الْعَدْلِ والإنصافِ، وَآمِنّي فيهِ مِنْ كُلّ ما أخافُ، بِعِصْمَتِكَ يا عِصْمَةَ الْخائِفينَ

Lord! Decorate me in it with a covering and with honors, shield me in it with the outfit of contentment and sufficiency, enable me in it to be just and fair, and bring me in it security against what I fear with Your protection, O Protector of the fearful!

Prayer tracker

Fajr ☐

Dhur ☐

Asr ☐

tarawih ☐

Maghrib ☐

Isha'a ☐

Nawafel ☐

Day 13

اَللّـهُمَّ طَهِّرْني فيهِ مِنَ الدَّنَسِ والأقذارِ، وَصَبِّرْني فيهِ عَلى كائِناتِ الأقدارِ، وَوَفِّقْني فيهِ لِلتُّقى وَصُحْبَةِ الأبرارِ، بِعَوْنِكَ يا قُرَّةَ عَيْنِ الْمَساكينَ

Lord! Purify me in it from uncleanness and filth,

enable me in it to be patient about whatever the

fates bring, grant me success in it for righteousness

and for the company of the kind ones with Your

assistance, O apple of the eyes of the indigent!

Prayer tracker

Fajr ☐

Dhur ☐

Asr ☐

tarawih ☐

Maghrib ☐

Isha'a ☐

Nawafel ☐

Day 14

اَللّـهُمَّ لا تُواخِذْني فيهِ بِالْعَثَراتِ، وَاَقِلْني فيهِ مِنَ الْخَطايا
وَالْهَفَواتِ ، وَلا تَجْعَلْني فيهِ غَرَضاً لِلْبَلايا والآفات،
بِعِزَّتِكَ يا عِزَّ الْمُسْلِمينَ

Lord! Do not penalize me in it when I slip,

protect me in it from sinning and slipping, and

do not be an object to trials and tribulations

with Your Dignity, O One Who safeguards the

dignity of the Muslims!

Prayer tracker

Fajr ☐

Dhur ☐

Asr ☐

tarawih ☐

Maghrib ☐

Isha'a ☐

Nawafel ☐

Day 15

اَللّٰهُمَّ ارْزُقْني فيهِ طاعَةَ الْخاشِعينَ، وَاشْرَحْ فيهِ
صَدْري بِإِنابة الْمُخْبِتينَ، بأمانك يا أمان
الْخائِفِينَ

Lord! Grant me in it the obedience of the devout,

expand my chest in it with the return to You of

those who abandoned You, through Your security,

O One Who brings security to the fearful!

Prayer tracker

Fajr ☐

Dhur ☐

Asr ☐

tarawih ☐

Maghrib ☐

Isha'a ☐

Nawafel ☐

Day 16

اَللّـهُمَّ وَفِّقْني فيهِ لِمُوافَقَةِ الأبرارِ، وَجَنِّبْني فيهِ مُرافَقَةَ الأشرارِ، وَآوِني فيهِ بِرَحْمَتِكَ إلى دارِ الْقَرارِ، بِإلهيّتِكَ يا إلـهَ الْعالَمينَ

Lord! Grant me success in it to be in agreement with the kind ones, enable me in it to avoid the company of evildoers, enable me in it with Your mercy to be lodged in the abode of eternity with Your Godhead, O Lord of the Worlds!

Prayer tracker

Fajr ☐

Dhur ☐

Asr ☐

tarawih ☐

Maghrib ☐

Isha'a ☐

Nawafel ☐

Day 17

اَللّـهُمَّ اهْدِني فيهِ لِصالِحِ الإعمال، وَاقْضِ لي فيهِ الْحَوائِجَ وَالآمال، يا مَنْ لا يَحْتاجُ إِلَى التَّفْسيرِ وَالسُّؤالِ، يا عالِماً بِما في صُدُورِ الْعالَمينَ، صَلِّ عَلى مُحَمَّد وَآلِهِ الطّاهِرينَ

Lord! Grant me in it guidance to do good deeds,

allot for me in it the fulfillment of needs and of

aspirations, O One Who needs no explanation or

queries, the One Who knows the innermost of the

worlds, bless Muhammed and his pure Progeny!

Prayer tracker

Fajr ☐

Dhur ☐

Asr ☐

tarawih ☐

Maghrib ☐

Isha'a ☐

Nawafel ☐

Day 18

اَللّـهُمَّ نَبِّهْني فيهِ لِبَرَكاتِ أسحارِه، وَنَوِّرْ فيهِ قَلْبي بِضِياءِ
أنوارِه، وَخُذْ بِكُلِّ أعضائي إِلَى إِتْباعِ آثارِه، بِنُورِكَ يا
مُنَوِّرَ قُلُوبِ الْعارِفينَ

Lord! Make me attentive in it to the blessings of

his Sahar times, enlighten my heart in it with the

light of its noors, make all my parts follow its

tracks with Your own Noor, O One Who brings the

noor (light) to the hearts of those who know You!

Prayer tracker

Fajr ☐

Dhur ☐

Asr ☐

tarawih ☐

Maghrib ☐

Isha'a ☐

Nawafel ☐

Day 19

اللّهُمّ وَفّر فِيهِ حَظّي مِنْ بَرَكَاتِهِ، وَسَهّلْ سَبِيلِي إِلَى خَيْرَاتِهِ،
وَلا تَحْرِمْنِي قَبُولَ حَسَنَاتِهِ، يَا هَادِياً إِلَى الحَقّ المُبِينِ

Lord! on this day, please save me a share of its

blessings; And make my way easy to the obtainment

of its goodness, do not deprive me of the acceptance of

its good deeds, O He Who guides to the evident truth

Prayer tracker

Fajr ☐

Dhur ☐

Asr ☐

tarawih ☐

Maghrib ☐

Isha'a ☐

Nawafel ☐

Day 20

اَللّـٰهُمَّ افْتَحْ لي فيهِ أبواب الْجِنانِ، وأغلق عَنّي فيهِ أبواب النّيرانِ، وَوَفِّقْني فيهِ لِتِلاوَةِ الْقُرْآنِ، يا مُنْزِلَ السَّكينَةِ فى قُلُوبِ الْمُؤْمِنينَ

Lord! Open for me in it the gates of the gardens,
close from me in it the gates of the fires, enable me
in it to recite the Qur'an, O One Who sends down
calm to the hearts of the faithful!

Prayer tracker

Fajr ☐

Dhur ☐

Asr ☐

tarawih ☐

Maghrib ☐

Isha'a ☐

Nawafel ☐

Day 21

اَللَّهُمَّ اجْعَلْ لى فيهِ إلى مَرْضاتِكَ دَليلاً، وَلا تَجْعَلْ

لِلشَّيْطانِ فيهِ عَلَيَّ سَبيلاً، وَاجْعَلِ الْجَنَّةَ لى مَنْزِلاً وَمَقيلاً،

يا قاضِيَ حَوائِجِ الطّالِبينَ

Lord! Guide me in it to earn Your Pleasure, do not

let Satan find in it his way to me, and let Paradise

be my home and eternal abode, O One Who fulfills

the needs of those who plead!

Prayer tracker

Fajr ☐

Dhur ☐

Asr ☐

tarawih ☐

Maghrib ☐

Isha'a ☐

Nawafel ☐

Day 22

اَللّـهُمَّ افْتَحْ لى فيهِ أبواب فَضْلِكَ، وَاَنْزِلْ عَلَيَّ فيهِ بَرَكاتِكَ، وَوَفِّقْني فيهِ لِمُوجِباتِ مَرْضاتِكَ، وَاَسْكِنّي فيهِ بُحْبُوحاتِ جَنّاتِكَ، يا مُجيبَ دَعْوَةِ الْمُضْطَرّينَ

Lord! Open for me in it the gates of Your favor, send down to me in it Your blessings, enable me in it to earn whatever brings about Your Pleasure, house me in it in the opulence of Your gardens, O One Who responds to the call of the compelled ones!

Prayer tracker

Fajr ☐

Dhur ☐

Asr ☐

tarawih ☐

Maghrib ☐

Isha'a ☐

Nawafel ☐

Day 23

اَللّـهُمَّ اغْسِلْني فيهِ مِنَ الذُّنوبِ، وَطَهِّرْني فيهِ مِنَ
الْعُيُوبِ، وَامْتَحِنْ قَلْبي فيهِ بِتَقْوَى الْقُلُوبِ، يا مُقيلَ
عَثَراتِ الْمُذْنِبينَ

Lord! Wash my sins away in it, purify me

from defects, ascertain my heart in it with the

piety of the hearts, O One Who corrects the

slips of the sinners!

Prayer tracker

Fajr ☐

Dhur ☐

Asr ☐

tarawih ☐

Maghrib ☐

Isha'a ☐

Nawafel ☐

Day 24

اَللّـهُمَّ إني أسألك فيهِ ما يُرْضيكَ، وأعوذ بِكَ مِمّا
يُؤْذيكَ، وأسألك التَّوْفيقَ فيهِ لِاَنْ أطيعك وَلا أعصيك،
يا جَوادَ السّائِلينَ

Lord! I plead to You to enable me to achieve

whatever pleases You, I seek refuge with You from

whatever offends You, and I plead to You to grant

me the ability to obey You and not to disobey, O most

Generous One of all those to whom pleas are made!

Prayer tracker

Fajr ☐

Dhur ☐

Asr ☐

tarawih ☐

Maghrib ☐

Isha'a ☐

Nawafel ☐

Day 25

اَللَّـهُمَّ اجْعَلْني فيهِ مُحِبًّا لأوليائِكَ، وَمُعادِياً
لأعدائِكَ، مُسْتَنّاً بِسُنَّةِ خاتَمِ أنبيائِكَ، يا عاصِمَ
قُلُوبِ النَّبِيّينَ

Lord! Make me in it one who loves Your friends,
who is hostile to Your foes, following the Sunnah of
the Seal of Your Prophets, O One Who protects the
prophets' hearts!

Prayer tracker

Fajr ☐

Dhur ☐

Asr ☐

tarawih ☐

Maghrib ☐

Isha'a ☐

Nawafel ☐

Day 26

اَللّـهُمَّ اجْعَلْ سَعْيِي فيهِ مَشْكُوراً، وَذَنْبِي فيهِ
مَغْفُوراً وَعَمَلي فيهِ مَقْبُولاً، وَعَيْبِي فيهِ مَسْتُوراً،
يا أَسْمَعَ السّامِعينَ

Lord! Make my endeavor in it appreciated (by You),
my sin it forgiven, my deed in it accepted, my defect
in it covered, O most hearing of those who hear
(pleas)!

Prayer tracker

Fajr ☐

Dhur ☐

Asr ☐

tarawih ☐

Maghrib ☐

Isha'a ☐

Nawafel ☐

Day 27

اَللّـهُمَّ ارْزُقْني فيهِ فَضْلَ لَيْلَةِ الْقَدْرِ، وَصَيِّرْ أموري
فيهِ مِنَ الْعُسْرِ إلى الْيُسْرِ، وَاقْبَلْ مَعاذيري، وَحُطَّ
عَنّي الذَّنْبَ وَالْوِزْرَ، يا رَؤوفاً بِعِبادِهِ الصّالِحينَ

Lord! Grant me in it the honor of Laylatul-Qadr,

change my affairs in it from hardship to ease, accept

my excuses, remove from the sin and its burden, O One

Who is affectionate towards His righteous servants!

Prayer tracker

Fajr ☐

Dhur ☐

Asr ☐

tarawih ☐

Maghrib ☐

Isha'a ☐

Nawafel ☐

Day 28

اَللّـهُمَّ وَفِّرْ حَظّي فيهِ مِنَ النَّوافِلِ، وأكرمني فيهِ بإحضارِ الْمَسائِلِ، وَقَرِّبْ فيهِ وسيلتي إليك مِنْ بَيْنِ الْوَسائِلِ، يا مَنْ لا يَشْغَلُهُ إلحاحُ الْمُلِحّينَ

Lord! Make my lot of Nafl (supererogatory) deeds in it abundant, honor me in it with the presence of pleas, bring my means towards You closer from among all means, O One Who is not distracted by the persistence of those who persist!

Prayer tracker

Fajr ☐

Dhur ☐

Asr ☐

tarawih ☐

Maghrib ☐

Isha'a ☐

Nawafel ☐

Day 29

اَللّـهُمَّ غَشِّني فيهِ بِالرَّحْمَةِ ، وَارْزُقْني فيهِ التَّوْفيقَ
وَالْعِصْمَةَ ، وَطَهِّرْ قَلْبي مِنْ غَياهِبِ التُّهْمَةِ ، يا
رَحيماً بِعِبادِهِ الْمُؤْمِنينَ

Lord! Overwhelm me in it with (Your) mercy, grant

me in it success and protection, purge my heart of the

depths of accusation, O most Merciful One of His

believing servants!

Prayer tracker

Fajr ☐

Dhur ☐

Asr ☐

tarawih ☐

Maghrib ☐

Isha'a ☐

Nawafel ☐

Day 30

اَللّـهُمَّ اجْعَلْ صِيامى فيهِ بِالشُّكْرِ وَالْقَبُولِ عَلى ما تَرْضاهُ
وَيَرْضاهُ الرَّسُولُ، مُحْكَمَةً فُرُوعُهُ بِالْأُصُولِ، بِحَقِّ سَيِّدِنا
مُحَمَّد وَآلِهِ الطّاهِرينَ، وَالْحَمْدُ للهِ رَبِّ الْعالَمينَ

*Lord! Make my fast in it a means to thanking You
and to accepting what You accept and what the
Messenger () accepts, its branches perfected through
its principles, by the right of our Master Muhammed
and his Pure Progeny, and all praise belongs to Allah,
Lord of the Worlds*

Prayer tracker

Fajr ☐

Dhur ☐

Asr ☐

tarawih ☐

Maghrib ☐

Isha'a ☐

Nawafel ☐

Made in the USA
Middletown, DE
07 May 2022

65448477R00022